# Seeds and Fruit

Melanie Waldron

Raintree is an imprint of Capstone Global Library Limited, a company incorporated in England and Wales having its registered office at 7 Pilgrim Street, London, EC4V 6LB – Registered company number: 6695582

**www.raintreepublishers.co.uk**
myorders@raintreepublishers.co.uk



Edited by Sian Smith and Adrian Vigliano
Designed by Cynthia Akiyoshi
Original illustrations © HL Studios
Illustrated by HL Studios
Picture research by Mica Brancic
Originated by Capstone Global Library Ltd
Printed in China by CTPS

ISBN 978 1 406 27480 6
17 16 15 14 13
10 9 8 7 6 5 4 3 2 1

**British Library Cataloguing in Publication Data**
Waldron, Melanie
Seeds and fruit (Plant parts)
A full catalogue record for this book is available from the British Library.

**Acknowledgements**
We would like to thank the following for permission to reproduce photographs: Alamy pp. 26 (© Alaska Stock/Joe Stock), 28 bottom (© Jeff Greenberg "0 people images"); Capstone Publishers pp. 13, 24, 25 (© Karon Dubke); Getty Images p. 27 bottom (UIG/Auscape); Naturepl.com pp. 4 (© Fabio Liverani), 11, 18 bottom (© Nature Production), 14 (© Dietmar Nill), 15 (© Fabrice Cahez), 21 (© Doug Wechsler), 17 top (© Visuals Unlimited), 27 top (© Jack Dykinga); Proceedings of the National Academy of Sciences p. 23; Shutterstock pp. 5 (© 2009fotofriends), 7 (© Elliotte Rusty Harold), 9 (© Alexandra Giese), 10 (© Vitaly Ilyasov), 12 (© Denis Vrublevski), 16 (© HHelene), 19 (© Peter Wollinga), 22 (© Bogdan Wankowicz), 29 (© n7atal7i), 29 (© Yai), 17 bottom (© Ethan Daniels), 18 top (© Videowokart), 28 top (© nexus 7), 8 top (© Madlen), Imprint page (© Ammit Jack), Title page (© elxeneize).

Cover photograph reproduced with permission of Shutterstock (© elxeneize).

We would like to thank Michael Bright for his invaluable help in the preparation of this book.

# Contents


| | |
|---|---|
| Seeds and fruits galore! | 4 |
| Parts of flowering plants | 6 |
| Becoming a seed | 8 |
| Not just for eating! | 10 |
| Try this! | 12 |
| Delicious fruits | 14 |
| Wind, water, and walking | 16 |
| Dropping, shaking, and bursting | 18 |
| Inside a seed | 20 |
| A new plant | 22 |
| Try this! | 24 |
| Seeds and fruits around the world | 26 |
| Seeds, fruits, and us | 28 |
| Glossary | 30 |
| Find out more | 31 |
| Index | 32 |


Some words are shown in bold, **like this**. You can find out what they mean by looking in the glossary.

# Seeds and fruits galore!

When you think of seeds and fruits, what comes to mind? You can probably think of lots of different fruits and seeds that you can eat. You may also have planted seeds to grow plants and flowers. You may know that farmers around the world use millions of seeds to plant and grow **crops**. But have you ever wondered what seeds and fruit actually are, or how they are made?

There are lots of different kinds of fruits you can eat. Have you ever wondered why plants make fruits?

All of these beautiful flowers are there to make seeds.

## New plants

Seeds and fruits are made by plants. They are made by the flowers that grow on the plant. Seeds can be found inside fruits. When they are removed from the plant, they can grow into new plants. There are lots of different kinds of fruits and seeds.

All flowering plants make fruits and seeds. Even **broadleaved** trees grow flowers and make fruits and seeds.

### Collecting seeds

Lots of people collect seeds from garden flowers. They do this so they can plant the seeds where they would like those flowers to grow.

# Parts of flowering plants

For flowers to grow and make seeds, the plant needs other important parts. The **stem** of the plant supports the whole plant. The plant's leaves make food for the plant using sunlight and a gas from the air called **carbon dioxide**. The roots hold the plant in the ground. They take in water and **nutrients** from the soil. Flowers have special male parts and female parts. These work together to make seeds.

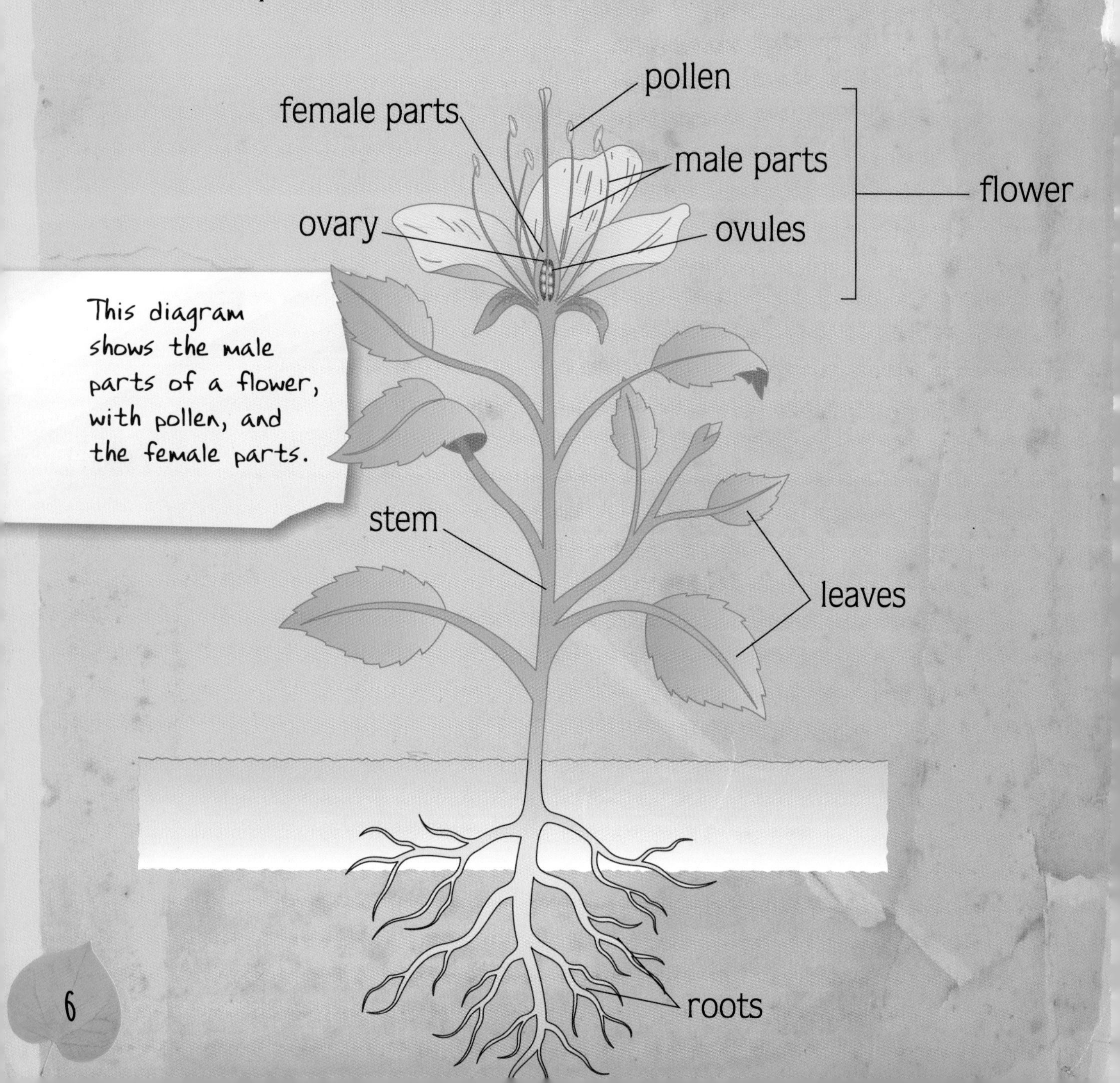


This diagram shows the male parts of a flower, with pollen, and the female parts.

## Flower to flower

The **pollen** from one flower has to move to the female part of the same kind of flower. It does this with the help of animals, and the wind. Insects, birds, and bats like to eat a sweet liquid called **nectar** in the flower. As they move from flower to flower, the animals transfer the pollen.

### Colours and smells

Flowers pollinated by animals are often brightly coloured, to attract the animals to them. Some of them give off scents to attract animals.

This honeybee has lots of pollen stuck to its legs. It will spread this pollen as it travels from flower to flower, pollinating each flower as it goes.

# Becoming a seed

When pollen lands on the female part of the flower, it grows a tube down into the **ovary** to the **ovules**. This is where the female bits of the seeds, called the ovum, are stored. Once the male bit of the seed from the pollen has joined with the ovum, it can grow into a seed. Some plants grow only one seed in each flower. Others can grow hundreds of seeds in every flower.

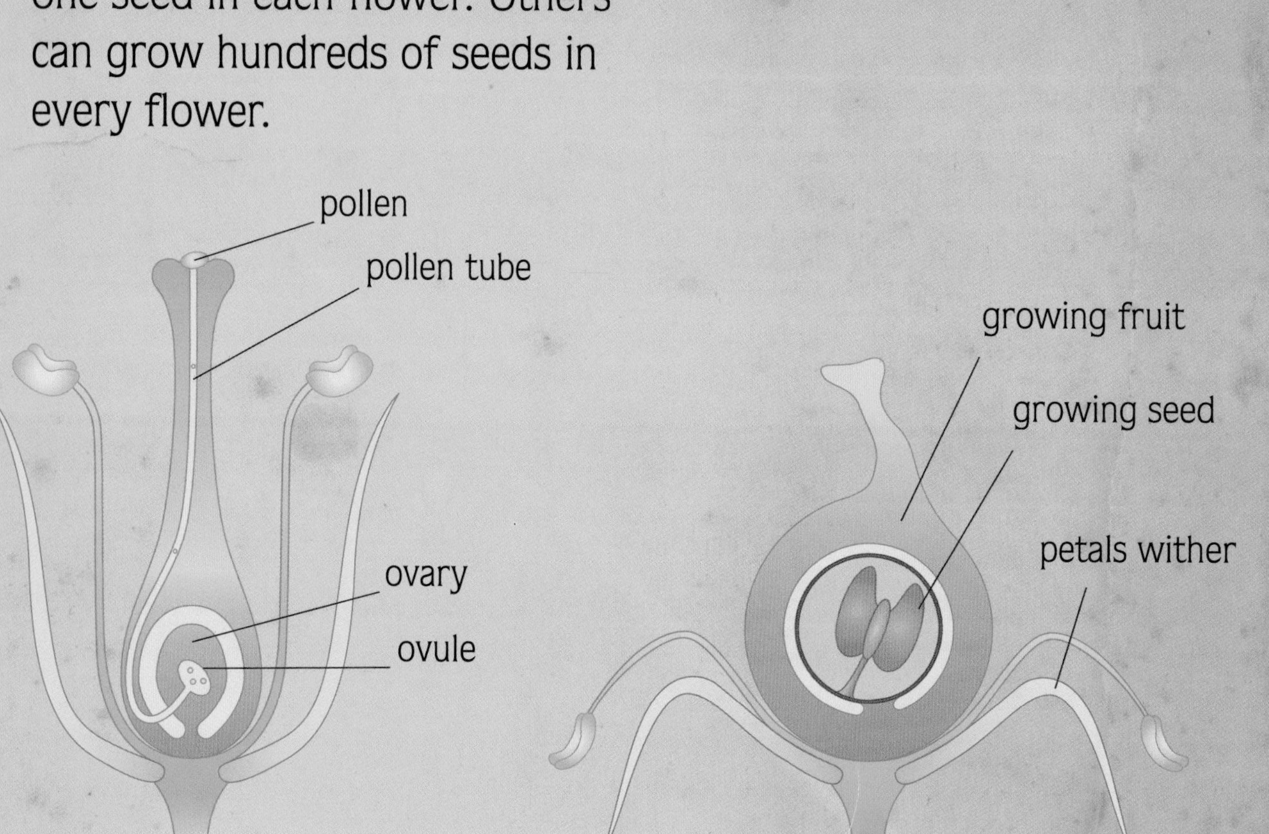


The diagram on the left shows the pollen growing a tube and reaching down to the ovule. The one on the right shows the flower dying and the seed growing.

This flower's petals are dying because seeds are growing inside it. The green part is the ovary, which swells as the seeds grow.

## Withering flowers

Once seeds are growing inside a flower, the flower's job is done. The petals dry up and drop off. As the seeds grow, the ovary around them protects them. This is the part of the plant that we call the fruit.

### Long tube

Some plants have very long female parts. This means that the pollen has to grow a long tube to reach the ovary. Corn pollen has to grow a tube about 20 centimetres (about 8 inches) long!

# Not just for eating!

Not all fruits are sweet and juicy! Their job is to protect the seeds and to help them move away from the plant. They have to move to a new space where they can grow into new plants.

## Wet fruits

We usually think of fruits as fleshy and juicy. Many of them certainly are, such as plums, apples, and raspberries. These fruits are called **succulent** fruits.

Many fruits are poisonous to humans but are enjoyed by other animals. Birds eat lots of different berries. This bird is eating mountain ash berries.

This pod on a Japanese violet plant has split open. The seeds are ripe and ready to make new plants.

## Dry fruits

Plant fruits can also be dry. For example, **nuts** are dry fruits with hard shells. Acorns and walnuts are dry fruits. **Achenes** are small, dry fruits. They sometimes have papery wings, such as sycamore seed fruits.

**Pods** are long, dry fruits with their seeds lined up in a row inside, such as pea pods. **Grains** are small dry fruits that are joined to seed shells, such as rice and wheat.

### Seeds without fruits

**Conifer** trees make seeds in their **cones**. The cones close up to protect the growing seeds. When the seeds are ready, the cones open up and the seeds flutter out.

# Try this!

See if you can find seeds inside some **edible** fruits – fruits that you can eat.

You will need:

- different edible fruits
- knife
- adult helper

1 Gather as many different fruits as you can. You could choose from a huge list, including apples, pears, oranges, lemons, limes, mangoes, grapes, melons, plums, cherries, grapefruits, peaches, passionfruits, lychees, and kiwi fruits. Don't forget that some things we think of as vegetables – such as tomatoes, courgettes, aubergines, and peppers – are actually fruits!

2 Very carefully, split the fruits apart to see if you can find the seed or seeds inside. You will be able to use your fingers on the softer fruits. You may need to ask an adult to help you cut the harder ones with a knife.

3

Count how many seeds are inside each fruit. This may be difficult with some fruits, for example kiwi. The seeds inside a kiwi are tiny, and there are a lot of them!

4

Compare the sizes of the seeds you have found. Some seeds, such as mango seeds, are very large.

5

Look at where the seeds are found in the fruit. Some are in the centre, surrounded by soft flesh that is quite hard to separate from the seed case. Others, such as apple seeds, are in little compartments inside the fruit.

## What next?

Create a display of your work. Take photographs of each fruit and its seeds and stick these on a sheet of paper. Label the photographs and write down the number of seeds you found in each fruit.

# Delicious fruits

Plants often grow fruits to help them move their seeds away to grow in a new place. Some plants do this by growing fruits that animals like to eat. These include all the fruits that humans like to eat. Animals pick the fruits from the plant and eat them. Tiny seeds are swallowed by the animals. The seeds pass through the animals and come out in their droppings. Larger seeds are simply dropped by the animals.

This bat is eating fruit. Any seeds that it swallows will pass through its stomach and come out in its faeces.

Animals store food to eat during the winter. A forgotten walnut can become a new tree in spring.

## Hiding fruits

Some animals take fruits and store them for later. Squirrels like to eat nuts. They bury some in the ground. If they forget about them, the nuts can grow into new plants.

## Bright berries

Berries, such as rosehips, are very brightly coloured. This is so birds can easily spot them as they fly past. The birds eat the berries, then fly off. The seeds pass out in the birds' droppings, often very far from the plant.

# Wind, water, and walking

The wind helps some plants scatter their seeds. Sycamore, dandelion, tufted vetch, ash, lime, willow, maple, and thistle seeds are carried by the wind. Many of these seeds are tiny and light, so the wind can carry them. Larger ones have papery "wings" or feathery "parachutes" to help them fly in the wind.

The seeds of rosebay willowherb plants have feathery parachutes that help them float on the wind.

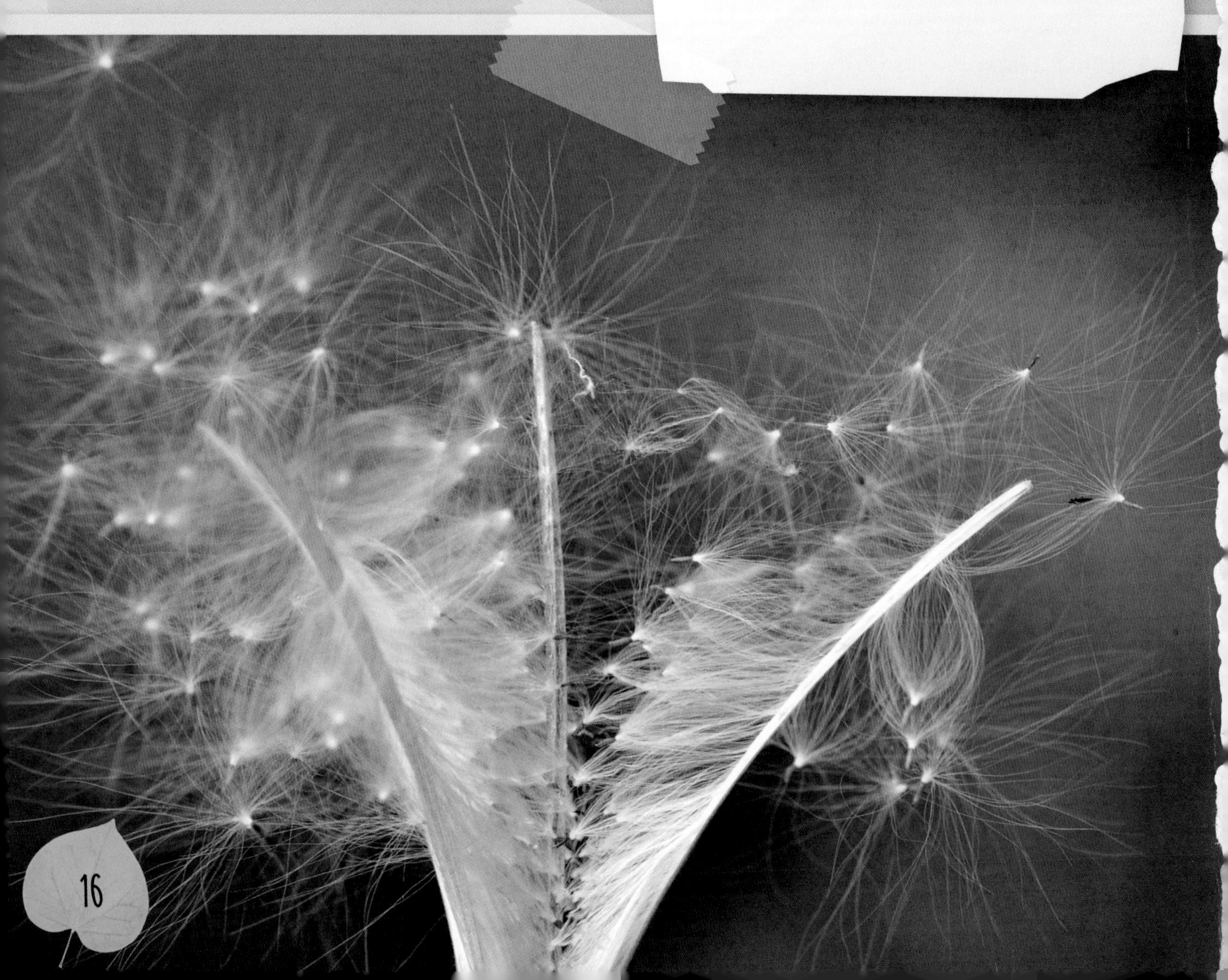

These burrs are sticking to the fur of a deer. They can be carried far from the parent plant in this way.

## Hitching and floating

Some plants have fruits that are designed to stick to animals' fur. Burdock fruits – called burrs – are covered in tiny hooks. They catch onto the fur of any passing animal. They are carried away, and later fall off or are scratched off by the animal. Some fruits can float on water.

### Floating away

Water lily fruits have a layer of air trapped inside them. This helps them to float away on the surface of the water. Coconuts have waterproof shells. They can float up to 2,000 kilometres (about 1,200 miles) away on the sea before reaching land.

# Dropping, shaking, and bursting

Have you ever seen an exploding plant? Some plants have fruits that simply burst open when the seeds are ready or when something brushes past them. The seeds fly out and land on the ground. Ripe peas burst out of their pods. Himalayan balsam fruits explode when you touch them.

Some plants have seeds that rattle about inside the fruits. The fruits have little holes that the seeds can fly out of. Poppy seeds fly out of the hard fruit capsule when the wind blows it.

This plant is sometimes called "touch-me-not"! When things brush against its seed pods, the pods burst open and fling their seeds out.

Very few of these sweet chestnut seeds will grow into large trees. Many will be eaten by animals.

## Falling and rolling

Some fruits just drop away from the plant. Horse chestnut trees drop their heavy fruits to the ground below. The parasol lily drops its flower head to the ground. It rolls about in the wind, scattering its seeds.

### Into the dark

Ivy-leaved toad-flax is an unusual plant that grows on walls. When its seeds are ripe, the stems grow towards dark cracks in the rocks. They push the seeds into these cracks, and the seeds start to grow there.

# Inside a seed

Plant fruits do the important job of getting the seeds to new places. Once there, the seeds can start to grow. They contain most of the things they need for this to happen.

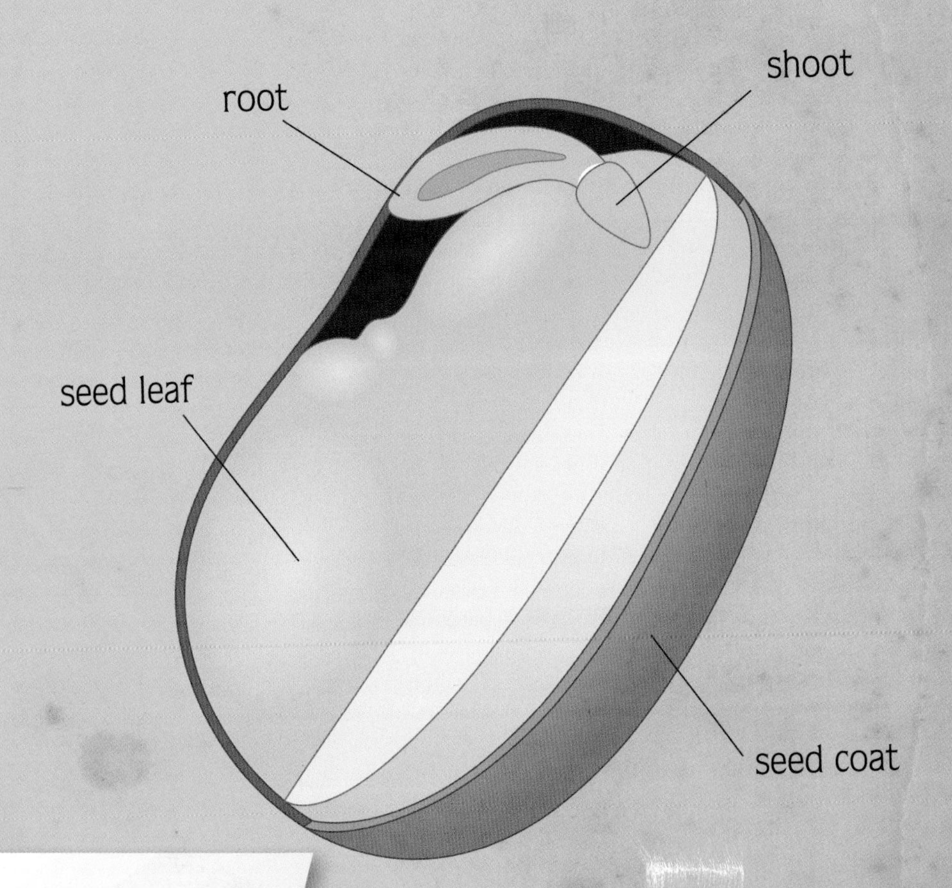


This diagram shows what is inside a seed. Even the tiniest seeds contain these things.

Inside each seed is a tiny new plant. There is also enough food to help this tiny plant grow and survive until it can grow leaves and make food for itself.

## Seed parts

The **seed coat** protects the tiny plant and stops insects from eating it. The root pushes through the seed coat and down into the ground. The shoot is the part of the plant that will push up above the ground and become the stem.

## Dried out

Most seeds contain very little water. This stops the tiny plant inside from going mouldy. The seed coat keeps water out, until the seed is ready to grow into a new plant.

The tiny plant has one or two **seed leaves**. These contain the food needed by the plant as it first starts to grow.

Some seeds from pods, like these black-eyed peas, have a little scar where they once attached to the pod. The scar is the white bit surrounded by black.

# A new plant

Seeds only begin to **germinate**, or start growing, when the time is right. They can lie in wait for a while until this happens. A seed needs the right amount of warmth, water, and **oxygen** before it can germinate. Some seeds can lie in wait for hundreds of years!

This is a germinating seed. The roots push downwards and the shoot pushes upwards.

When a seed germinates, it takes in water and oxygen through a tiny hole in its seed coat. Then the tiny root pushes out of the seed coat and down into the ground. This can take in water, so the plant can grow more.

## Ancient seeds

Seeds can lie in wait for a long time. Scientists found some seeds frozen deep in ice in Russia. They were about 32,000 years old. The scientists warmed them up – and they germinated!

## Pushing upwards

After the root comes out, the little shoot pushes up out of the seed. Some plants take their little seed leaves out of the ground with them, others leave them inside the seed.

Once the shoot has grown its first **true leaves**, the roots carry on growing down and the stem grows up. A new plant is made.

# Try this!

Try this experiment to see how different conditions affect how well a seed germinates.

You will need:

- three bean seeds
- cotton wool balls
- three plastic cups or dishes
- pen
- water
- fridge

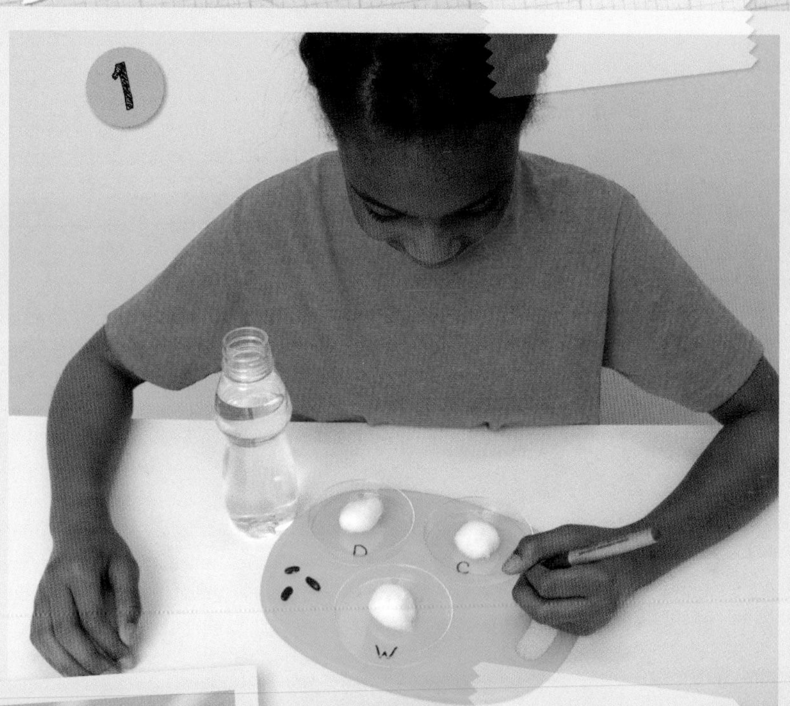


**1** Take three bean seeds. Put each one in a cotton wool ball, inside a plastic cup or dish. Keep one dry, and mark this with a "d". Add water to the other two so that the cotton wool balls are damp.

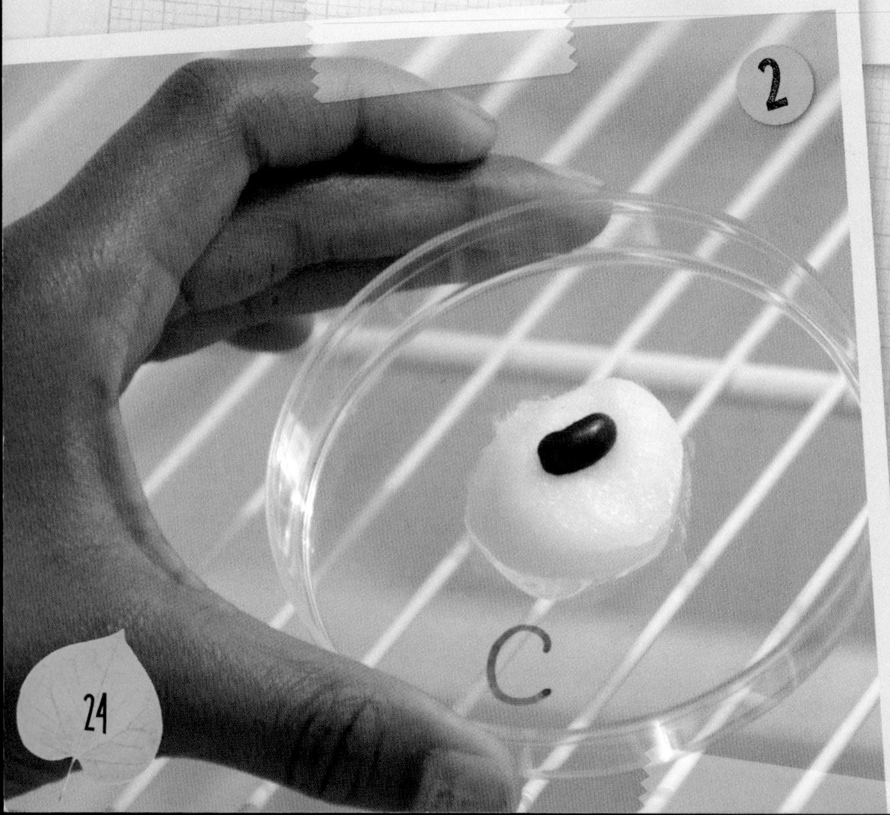


**2** Mark one of the dampened cups with the letter "c". This one should be kept in a cold place, such as a fridge.

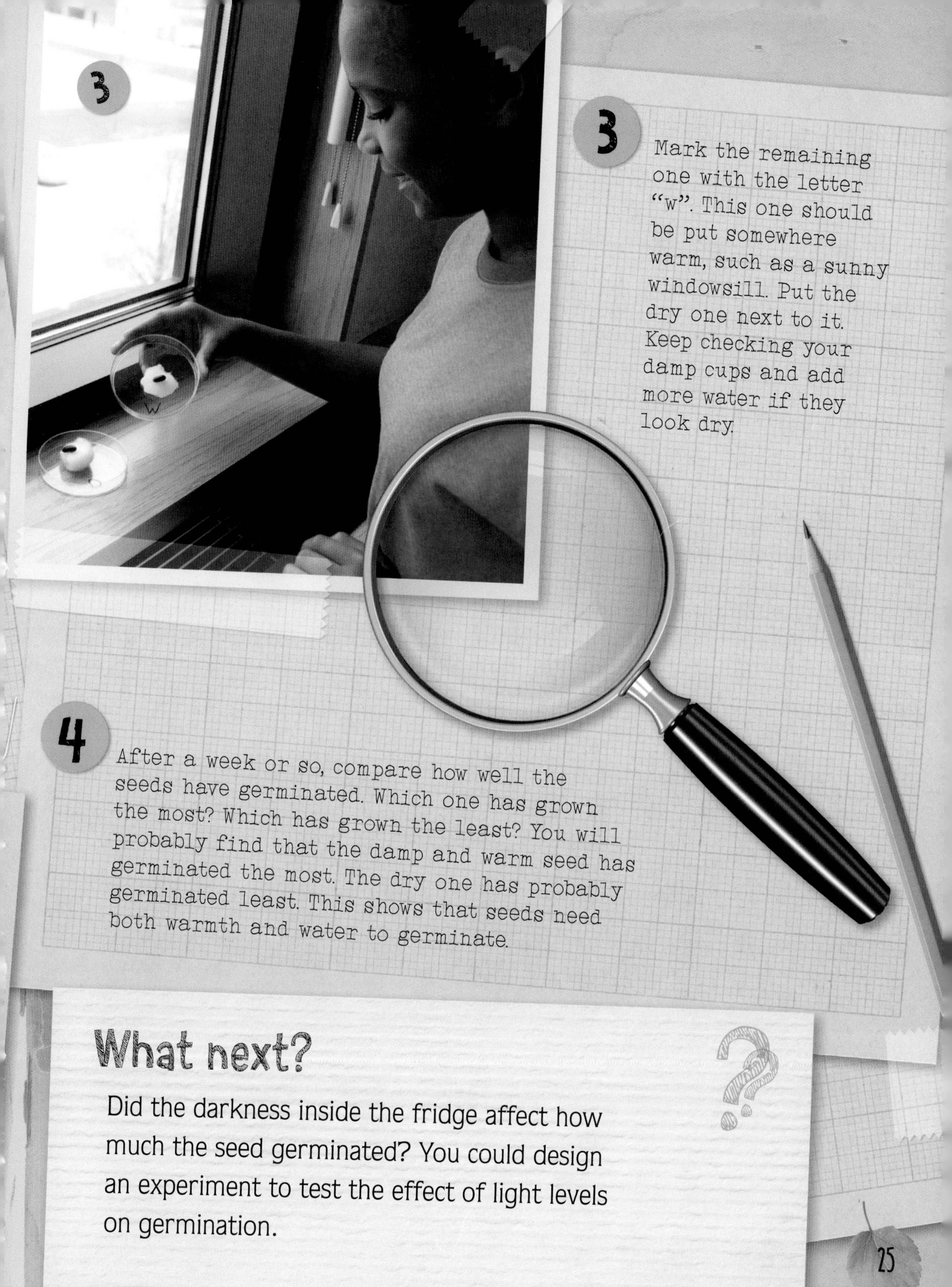


3 Mark the remaining one with the letter "w". This one should be put somewhere warm, such as a sunny windowsill. Put the dry one next to it. Keep checking your damp cups and add more water if they look dry.

4 After a week or so, compare how well the seeds have germinated. Which one has grown the most? Which has grown the least? You will probably find that the damp and warm seed has germinated the most. The dry one has probably germinated least. This shows that seeds need both warmth and water to germinate.

## What next?

Did the darkness inside the fridge affect how much the seed germinated? You could design an experiment to test the effect of light levels on germination.

# Seeds and fruits around the world

Plants grow, flower, and make seeds in most places in the world. Many grow in areas where conditions are difficult. They have **adapted** to be able to grow in these places.

The woolly lousewort's hairs are a special adaptation to its cold environment.

Some plants grow in the cold Arctic. The woolly lousewort has lots of little hairs around its flowers. These trap heat inside the flower. This is important, because its seeds can't develop at low temperatures.

## Waiting for rain

In some hot, dry deserts, there is very little water. Seeds can lie in wait for many years until there is rainfall. After enough rainfall they germinate, grow, and flower in a very short time. The desert becomes carpeted in colour. The flowers make new seeds that fall to the ground and again lie in wait for a rain shower.

### Fire please!

Banksias growing in Australia have tough wooden seed pods. They stay shut until a bush fire spreads through the area. After the fire, the pods open up and let the seeds drop onto the newly cleared ground.

# Seeds, fruits, and us

Fruits and seeds are very important to humans. They are a valuable and healthy food source. They also give us other products, such as oils. Sunflower seeds are crushed to make cooking oil. We also use olive oil from crushed olive fruits and peanut oil from crushed peanuts. Some oil can be used as fuel for vehicles.

This bus runs on a chemical called biodiesel, which is made partly from vegetable oil.

These seeds are used to make chocolate!

## Seeds, fruits, and farming

Around the world, farmers buy and sell seeds to plant and grow important crops. All the vegetarian food we eat comes from plants. The meat that we eat mostly comes from animals that eat plants.

### Sweet treats

Even chocolate is made using seeds! It is made using cocoa beans, the seeds of the cacao tree. These are roasted, ground, and pressed to get cocoa butter. This is mixed with milk and sugar to make chocolate.

# Glossary

**achene** small, dry, hard seed that is attached at a single point and does not split open when it is ripe

**adapt** change over time to suit the environment

**broadleaved** tree with flat, wide leaves rather than thin needles. Trees with needles are called conifers.

**carbon dioxide** gas with no colour or smell that is found in the air

**cone** hard, scaly container that grows on conifers and contains seeds

**conifer** tree with cones and narrow leaves called needles. Pines and firs are conifers.

**crop** plant grown on a farm, usually for food

**edible** can be eaten

**germinate** start to grow into a new plant

**grain** small, hard seed of a cereal plant, such as wheat or rice. Grain is used for food and is often ground up to make flour.

**nectar** sweet liquid made by plants to attract animals. When the animals eat the nectar, they gather pollen that they can then take to another flower.

**nut** dry seed or fruit made up of a kernel contained in a hard, tough shell. The kernel of nuts is often used as food.

**nutrient** chemical that helps plants to live and grow

**ovary** part of a flower that contains the ovule

**ovule** very small female cell in plants that develops into a seed when it is fertilized

**oxygen** gas with no colour or smell that makes up about one-fifth of air. Most living things need oxygen.

**pod** long, thin, firm pouch that contains the seeds of a pea or bean plant

**pollen** fine powder made in plant flowers. It is used by plants to fertilize flowers to make seeds.

**ripe** fully grown

**seed coat** tough covering on a seed that protects it from harm and stops it drying out

**seed leaf** one of usually two tiny leaves that form inside a seed and appear after a seed has germinated. Seed leaves are usually different shapes from the plant's leaves that grow later (true leaves).

**stem** main part of a plant that supports the branches, leaves, and flowers

**succulent** fleshy and juicy

**true leaves** leaves that a plant grows after it has germinated

# Find out more

## Books

*Fruit* (See How Plants Grow), Nicola Edwards (Wayland, 2012)

*Plants* (Wildlife Watchers), Terry Jennings (QED, 2010)

*Seeds, Bulbs, Plants, and Flowers* (Little Science Stars), Helen Orme (Ticktock, 2009)

*Zoom! The Invisible World of Plants*, Camilla de la Bedoyere (QED, 2012)

## Websites

**www2.bgfl.org/bgfl2/custom/resources_ftp/client_ftp/ks2/science/plants_pt2/dispersal.htm**

This website has animations that show different ways of seed dispersal.

**www.bbc.co.uk/nature/plants**

This website has lots of information about plants. There are also some amazing film clips of plants all around the world.

**www.nhm.ac.uk/education/online-resources/webquests/launch.php?webquest_id=5&partner_id=hist**

This website launches a "Fruit Challenge" activity where there is information about fruits, how they form, and what they are used for. There are lots of different activities.

## Places to visit

The Royal Botanic Gardens in Kew in London has plants from all over the world.

The Eden Project in Cornwall is a series of huge domed greenhouses, one of which contains a rainforest! There are fun activities and amazing things to learn about plants.

Go for a walk in your local nature park! Spend time looking closely at all the different seeds and fruits you can see.

# Index

achenes 11
adaptations 26
animals 7, 14, 15, 17, 29

banksias 27
bats 7
berries 10, 15
birds 7, 15
broadleaved trees 5
burrs 17

cacao trees 29
carbon dioxide 6
cones 11
conifer trees 11
corn 9
crops 4, 29

droppings 14, 15
dry fruits 11

edible fruits 12–13, 14, 28, 29

farmers 4, 29
female parts 6, 7, 8, 9
food 6, 20, 21, 28
frozen seeds 23
fuel 28

germination 22, 23, 24–25, 27
grains 11
Himalayan balsam fruits 18

leaves 5, 6, 20, 21, 23
male parts 6, 8

nectar 7
nutrients 6
nuts 11, 15, 28

oils 28
olives 28
ovaries 8, 9
ovules 8
oxygen 22

peanuts 28
peas 11, 18
pods 11, 18, 27
pollen 7, 8, 9
poppy seeds 18

rice 11
roots 6, 21, 22, 23
rosehips 15

scents 7
seed coats 21, 22
seed leaves 21, 23
shoots 21, 23
sunlight 6, 25
sycamore seeds 11, 16

temperatures 22, 23, 24, 25, 26
toad-flax plants 19
trees 5, 11, 19, 29

water 6, 17, 21, 22, 24, 25, 27
wet fruits 10
wheat 11
wind 7, 16, 18, 19